Death for Beginners
Chris Gerolmo

© 2014 by Chris Gerolmo.

All rights reserved. All reproduction or transmission is prohibited without consent of the author through Patcheny Press.

Previously published in ebook form.
Limited first printed edition.
ISBN 978-0-9745042-3-0

Printed in the U.S.A.

www.patcheny.com
www.chrisgerolmo.com

Death for Beginners

Foreword

My wife Joan died just about three years ago now. She'd had a terrible time for some years before that, and she did some things in her anger and her pain that just about drove me crazy, but I loved her. I loved her the way I tell my kids I love them every day: like two dump trucks full of gold.

About a year after she died, I started writing these little books *for Beginners,* a series of sort of children's books for grownups, primers about what the world looks like when stripped of both denial and illusion, when viewed naked and well-lit, as corpses are viewed. They're short, and divided into even shorter chapters, so that they can be read in brief sittings by people who have little time for reading, or who have lost the habit. People like me.

I wrote one called Atheism for Beginners, and one about the sad state my country is in called *Kleptocracy for Beginners*. Then I took on the subject of death, which in some ways I suppose is the underlying subject of all of them.

I wanted to write about death as it really is, about what happens to our bodies when we die — and sometimes to our families — and how little any of it has to do with the comforting stories we tell ourselves about it. I'm a Recovering Catholic, and I meant to use religious stories, myths, and folk tales, to say something about the ways in which they reveal our wishes about death, about all the ways we'd rather it went, but to use just the facts as I'd sadly had to learn them to describe the real world in all its awful glory.

If someone were to ask me what human life is at its essence, I'd say it comes in two parts: on the one hand, reality, the known and the knowable, that with which our first job in life is always to come to terms; and on the other the stories we tell ourselves about it, which for every good reason tend toward wish-fulfillment and fantasies of victory and survival. This is an attempt to look at the former — reality — without the distortions of the latter — illusion.

And yet it's also a love story.

Go figure.

A is for Angels.

I'm afraid I don't believe in an afterlife, or not in one that takes place anywhere other than here in reality, anyway. According to a CBS News poll conducted in 2005, though, 78% of all American adults do. Of course, that same poll also revealed that 56% of American women believe in ghosts, and that more than one out of four American adults under the age of 45 actually claim to have seen one. To someone who's philosophically committed exclusively to the real, that's astounding.

At the same time, it makes perfect sense that fantasy is so widely preferred to reality where death is concerned, as the immediate afterlife here in reality has so very little to recommend it. Here, the afterlife is characterized by things like Palor, Livor, Rigor, and Algor Mortis, respectively Latin for the paleness, color, stiffness, and coolness of death — that last an oddly beautiful phrase to my ear, for what it describes. For those of us who choose to be buried, there's embalming and interment. For those of us who choose cremation, there are a couple of hours in the oven, followed by many years in an overpriced urn on the mantel, or in the case of our local surfers here in L.A., maybe a reverential dispersal in the waves off Zuma Beach. For those of us unlucky enough to be left out in the woods, there are the many indignities of putrefaction, among them hide beetles, skin slippage, and the occasional theft of our bones by dogs. But alas, no angels. I'm sorry. For better and for worse, all the angels are here, amongst the living. Until she died, my wife was widely considered to be one of them.

I remember, in the last week of Joan's life, sitting at her bedside, singing her one of the many love songs I'd written her over the years, then looking at her — at her sallow complexion, at her deep-set eyes, at the hollows at her temples, at her wrists that were only bones and skin — and starting to cry. She knew what I was afraid of — that I wouldn't be able to raise the kids on my own, that I could never live up to the example she had set as a parent, that I couldn't make it without her — and she whispered, "You can do this, Chris." Damn, I thought. Damn. That's my wife, all right. She's dying, and she's comforting me.

B is for Burial.

It's currently estimated that about 50 billion people have lived and died throughout the course of man's history on the planet. Taking into account the fact that we've been getting bigger and stronger throughout that time — and only recently fatter — let's say their average weight at death was 80 pounds. That's four trillion pounds of human flesh and bone, much of it interred in the soil to be eaten by bugs or to become nutrients for plants, trees, and crops, and thus returned to the food chain that way, and some just left to dry up and blow away, becoming part of the atmosphere, and being inhaled by such creatures as wild boars hunting for truffles or young lovers on the banks of rivers getting themselves pregnant and causing their parents great pain. We're each made up of about seven billion billion billion atoms, so the likelihood that some of them had once been part of another human being is quite good. Given the amount of organic material we're talking about, the likelihood that you ate a bit of someone else in your last meal is pretty good too. In that sense at least, we really are all part of one another, and death itself makes every meal a kind of communion.[1]

Of course, it's fair to say that at some meals, we commune more than at others. On my first date with Joan, we ate at a Chinese restaurant in Beverly Hills called Joss, and I remember feeling terribly lucky that this beautiful, bright, warm, funny woman seemed to feel so much at home in my company, and I in hers. We stayed, chatting and laughing, until the place closed. On our second date, we went to a friend's 40th birthday, then back to my house, where I told her she was the first girl I'd gone out with since I'd gotten sober about a year before, and that, unlike in

---

[1] If you're a recently bereaved spouse, I don't expect that to be of any more comfort to you than it was to me. If you're a child though, it might pique your interest. Until a few years ago, whenever I told one of my kids an odd fact like that — my twin girls are now seven and my son nine — if they weren't completely sure I was telling the truth, they'd peer at me and ask, "Is that in real life?" That became one of my favorite questions, and it's the standard by which everything in this little book will be measured, "Is that in real life?" I think coming to terms with real life is such a big part of growing up that they might as well be one and the same thing, and growing up is always our #1 job, no matter how old we are.

my previous life, when I'd always jumped into things head-first, as they say, I wanted to go slowly. Not that I had matured or anything. It's just that the idea that I'd have to take my clothes off in front of someone I liked for the first time without any alcohol or drugs to lubricate my self-consciousness was quite daunting to me. So I suggested we try a 90-day sex-free schedule, to see if we really felt that strongly about each other, an idea I'd just heard about from my 40-year-old friend. Joan thought that sounded terribly wise, or pretended to, but she didn't want to go, and I didn't want to let her. So she stayed the night, although we each kept to our own sides of the bed. We lasted 'til morning, when we made love for the first time. Oh well. So it goes with schedules, I guess, when love walks in the room. It was less than a year later that I woke her at 3 a.m. and sat on the bench at the foot of the bed to play her this love song I'd just written for her on the guitar.

burning down this building
june 20, 2001

i was burning down this building
when you walked in through that door
i hid my gas can behind my back
i don't burn nothing anymore
i was pissing on the future
when you sneaked in from the past
you're not the first girl i ever let in here
but you may well be the last
now all my friends are hoping
that i don't burn you too
but i think i finally found the girl
with the juice to keep me cool
i was burning down this building
hell i was burning up the world
i was dying in my own holy war
now i'm just living for a girl
now i go to work each morning
and i race home every night
but i don't run from sirens no more
and i don't flinch at flashing lights
instead i find myself hoping
and baby this is true
that for just one more lucky morning
i'll get to wake up next to you

She loved it. She cried. She made me sing it again. In fact, Joan was the only reason I ever got serious about writing songs. I'd written a few when I met her — I'm a screenwriter by profession — but when she heard them she made me join a songwriting seminar and put together a band and get out there and play around town, and now I'm an Emmy-nominated singer-songwriter as well. She was relentlessly encouraging, to me and to everyone she knew. It's one of the many things I miss about her. To tell you the truth, I haven't written more than a handful of songs in the three years since she died.

Anyway, a few months later, we were in London at the opening of a James Bond movie. The party was in a public park the production had taken over, and there were hundreds of well-dressed people there as well as a terrific jazz band. One of the producers was an old friend of mine, and she was trying to get people out on the dance floor they'd installed in the middle of the park, no doubt at great expense. I asked Joan to dance, so we walked out onto the empty dance floor to what we used to call in the eighth grade a "slow song." No one else joined us at all. At first, Joan was intensely self-conscious, feeling that all eyes were on her (they were). But soon enough she relaxed, and gave herself over to the music, and the feeling of being held, and of being loved, and so did I, and we whispered silly things to each other, and danced, and were transported. It must have been pretty clear that we were a couple of grownups in love, because when the song ended and we applauded the band, they stopped and applauded us in return.

C is for Cremation.

Joan died the day after Christmas 2007, after a long struggle with cancer. She had chosen to be cremated, so her body was sent by the undertaker to a local crematorium, where she was burned at between 1800 and 2100 degrees for about two hours in what's called a retort — a computer-controlled fire chamber lined with refractory bricks that resist heat. While bodies have been burned throughout history for various reasons, most notably on Hindu funeral pyres in India and on the occasional Catholic bonfire in

Europe or America (although in the latter case the burnees were generally not yet dead) cremation has only become popular in the West as an alternative to burial in the last 100 years. In fact, Pope Paul VI didn't lift the ban on cremation for Catholics — dead Catholics, that is — until 1963. Cremation is still forbidden to Jews, on the grounds that the souls of the recently dead are not yet aware that they're dead, and experience great pain at seeing their bodies be burned.

To tell you the truth, I didn't know until yesterday that the blue ceramic urn we bought from the funeral home to hold Joan's ashes held not her ashes, but rather about four pounds of her dried bones that had been pulverized by a device called an Electric Cremated Remains Processor into a kind of fine sand. Apparently there are no ashes left after cremation. The fire's too hot. There's only bone. Why people in the death business don't tell this to the bereaved I don't know, but it doesn't surprise me. When death is concerned, most people seem willing to smile and nod and let us think whatever we want to think.

Of course, Joan and I did the same thing when we got married. We realized with just a week or two to go that the state of California hadn't finalized Joan's divorce from her first husband yet — she'd filed the papers a year earlier and it should only have taken six months — so we had to decide whether to call the ceremony off or let it be just that: a ceremony. Which is what we did, in the end. We let everyone think it was legal, but it wasn't. It was just a show for the families.

Joan was terribly afraid about hers, too. I can still see it in her eyes in all the wedding pictures. She was worried about how they'd get along, especially her long-divorced but still-bitter mother with her father, but also whether or not they'd approve of her choice — her mother was a Daughter of the American Revolution and I'm only an Adult Child of Alcoholics. I told her what my therapist told me: when you're up there saying your vows, creating the new family you've actually chosen to create, you can finally look out at the crazy people you'd accidentally been born with and think, "Bye bye!"

But it didn't help. She still looked like a deer caught in the headlights. I don't think it was until I kissed her awake at the Four Seasons the next morning, and whispered, "Good morning, Mrs. Gerolmo," that she finally relaxed and let herself enjoy the whole thing. That's when she cried the traditional tears of joy. She told me for years thereafter that that was the first moment when she really felt married.

Her son Eddy moved in with us shortly after the wedding. He was six at the time, and a lovely kid with a rare sense of humor. Once, when his young cousin Liam, who's a bit of a terror, was stomping around barefoot in a huge box of Legos that the other kids had been playing with, some grownup asked what Liam was doing, and Eddy muttered, "Making Lego wine?" We got him into the local public school, and Joan started volunteering at the library, and making friends amongst the neighbors (I didn't know any of them) and meeting other moms at the park, and generally introducing me to the community I'd already been a part of for some ten years without ever really knowing it.

D is for Denial.

I said that when it comes to death, most people seem willing to let us think whatever we want to think. Not so the in-laws. Almost immediately after my wife's death, they began in one way and another denying to the children the fact that she was dead. They told the kids — my son was six and my daughters four at the time — that their mom would always be with them, that she was watching them from heaven, and that she still loved them very much. I have no doubt that she would have been with them, or watching them, or loving them, if she could. She was a wonderful mother. But she was dead, and to imply otherwise was a disservice to the kids, not to mention confusing. I remember a friend of mine talking about his dad, who died while on a business trip when my friend was seven. He was told so many times and so matter-of-factly that his dad had only gone to heaven that for years he thought heaven was some other little town in Idaho and that it was just a matter of time before he came back.

In these kinds of situations, of course, grown-ups think they're protecting children from the pain of reality, when in fact they're only indulging their own wishes to deny the abrupt permanence of death and the terrible facts of loss and sorrow. Me, I try to avoid denial whenever I can. As a recovering alcoholic — I'll be sober 12 years in February — I try to root it out in my own life as a matter of survival. Of course, it's fair to say that most recovering alcoholics believe in a god of some kind. Apparently, the connection between denial and faith that seems so obvious and scary to me doesn't faze them in the slightest. In my opinion, if denial is the ability to look directly at a thing we don't wish to see and not see it, then faith is the ability to see things that aren't there simply because we wish they were.

In any case, I held my tongue with the in-laws out of politeness — or such is my recollection anyway; I may actually be in denial about that, too — then later, when the kids asked where Mommy was, I explained to them what had really happened. Or tried to. I told them she died. Like the animals on Animal Planet. Like the rats and birds the cats bring home. They knew what that meant. But they still asked, "But where is she? Where did she go?" So I showed them her ashes — or her dried ground bones, anyway — and told them she'd been cremated, which didn't hurt because she was already dead, and we sat with her bones in their blue urn by the fireplace, and we clung together, and stared at them in silence. We felt her absence quite acutely, in that moment, and were terribly, terribly sad.[2]

By way of finishing the wedding story, though, we went to the Palm a few weeks later, Joan and I and Eddy, inviting as witnesses the friend who'd gotten a license online to perform the original ceremony and another couple, and signed the document that meant we were legally married. I prepared a document for Eddy to sign, too. It read, "Sept. 1, 2001. I hereby accept the unavoidable fact that Chris Gerolmo, aka Crispy, will now and forever, or until I'm 18 and I can run away to the jungle to become an ornithologist, be my stepfarter. Uh, step-farther. Sorry. Stepfather. As if I ever had any choice after Mommy first spotted him. Sincerely, Eddy." But the city of Beverly Hills managed to lose this paperwork, too. So it wasn't until our third try, when we went to the Office of the County Clerk together and stood on line holding hands like all the other couples, and did it all on the spot, that Joan and I were officially man and wife.

---

[2] We're not so sad to see them, now. In fact, it's nice to have them around. Whenever we have "Family Sleep in the Living Room Night," for instance — a tradition started by Joan — the kids fight for the right to sleep next to her, meaning to be on the mattress closest to the fireplace-surround on which rests the blue ceramic urn. It's a wonderful way to service the kids' wishes to have their mom be present even after her death and still be "in real life."

E is for Eternal Life.

By any standard, we were old for newlyweds — Joan 37 and I 48 — but we were also youthful, if not positively childish, and at the time I guess we expected to live forever, in the same silly way that everybody in love expects to live forever, or at least for what they call the foreseeable future, as if any of it really were. But if you'd asked us if we believed in Eternal Life, we would each have answered with a resounding No. I'm afraid Eternal Life is an idea whose future is not nearly as bright as its past.

In the Middle Ages, the Roman Catholic Church used it to rule Europe, side by side with its kings. The kings had the power to collect taxes and raise armies, but the Church controlled the story of the world — the story that justified the kings' power, that gave unto Caesar what is Caesar's — and used it (along with torture and dismemberment; remember the Inquisition?) to keep the peasants in line. The story it told is that in return for a life of poverty and hard labor here on earth, the faithful could expect an Eternal Life of leisure in heaven. Well, things have changed. The Renaissance broke the Church's exclusive hold on the public's imagination, and now, in twenty-first-century America, the Catholic Church is no more than a rich but irrelevant haven for pederasts, and most young people expect an eternal life of leisure here on earth in return for just getting into college.

I was looking through some of the things I saved from our wedding today, wondering if there was any reference to the Eternal in what we wrote for ourselves to say — there wasn't — and I came across something I'd completely forgotten about. As part of the ceremony, we quoted Arthur Miller on the subject of the play: "My conception of the audience is of a public each member of which is carrying about with him what he thinks is an anxiety, or a hope, or a preoccupation which is his alone and which isolates him from mankind; and in this respect at least the function of a play is to reveal him to himself so that he may touch others by virtue of the revelation of his mutuality with them." Joan and I then said this:

CHRIS

So every man has a secret that he believes separates him from the community of men.

JOAN

Maybe it's also the job of a wedding to show him that his secret is just like everyone else's.

CHRIS

My secret was that I knew I'd always be alone. I knew I'd always be unhappy. I had given up on love.

JOAN

And I was sure I'd never find it. So I hid from life.

CHRIS

And then I met Joan.

JOAN

And I met Chris.

CHRIS

And I came to realize that everything I'd believed about myself and my fate was wrong.

JOAN

And I found out that I hadn't known the first thing about love.

CHRIS

And now I have a new secret.

JOAN

Me, too.

I love that. It breaks my heart, but I love it. It reminds me of how happy and resolute we were, and that even though I feel that same way once again — that I've somehow been abandoned to a life of loneliness and sorrow — that I may well be as wrong now as I was then. In any case, the wedding took place right out here on the patio. We asked Eddy to be the ring-bearer but he'd done that job at his uncle's wedding the year before and didn't want to do it again. So we gave him a free hand. He decided to lead the procession in from the driveway, blowing bubbles as he marched. He was the Bubble Boy, and a huge hit amongst the guests. As far as I'm concerned, every wedding should have one.

My friend Dan gave the best man's speech, turning a tiny moment into a funny 15-minute story about meeting Joan for the first time in Manhattan just after I had gotten a very short haircut. When I left them together on the street for a moment to duck in somewhere and get something, he looked at her and said that with my new hairdo I looked more like a serial killer than ever before. Joan beamed and said, "I know. Isn't he cute?" Dan just stared, and nodded, and thought, "He's finally found the right girl."

F is for Post-Mortem Flatulence.

Johnny Carson once said, "For three days after death, hair and fingernails continue to grow, but phone calls taper off." Believe it or not, gas is still a problem in the afterlife, too. The sound of a loud fart at night has terrified many a medical student doing a rotation in the morgue, and apparently even more incapacitating is the sight of a recently dead cadaver when post-mortem gas production in the intestines causes it to grunt and sit up. In fact, post-mortem gas production plays a significant role in nature's response to death. It's the way maggots and other carrion-feeders are called to the meal. It's nature's version of the dinner bell. But we'll come back to that. I only mention it here because I have a story.

Years before Joan died, her old Carolina dog, Piggy, had a stroke and went blind — we only found out when she walked right into the pool one day and nearly drowned — and my wife made the hard decision to put her down. We took her to the vet's, and sat with her as she lay on the table, and the doctor gave her a massive shot of sedatives. Of course, Piggy was a magnificent dog, and a fighter, and this supposedly fatal cocktail only put her to sleep, and after about 20 minutes of listening to her snore, I went to find the doctor again. She gave Piggy another shot, this one even more massive. Piggy just went on snoring, and after a while Joan and I started to giggle. We'd been there most of an hour, holding hands across a table with a sizable dog between us, trying to take the task of ushering her out of this life as seriously as it deserved to be taken, and we were failing. We got the doctor again, and she gave Piggy a third shot, and finally, after several more minutes of snoring, and a long slow audible passing of gas that made us both laugh like little kids, Piggy died.

I'm not a dog person, but I knew how much Joan loved Piggy, so I'd been happy to have her come and live out her last days with us. But I was always a little leery of puppies. Before we were married, Joan had been actively campaigning for one, but at the time she was also actively campaigning for a baby. She had already made it clear to me that what she really wanted was a family in which the children outnumbered the adults. I assured her that even when it was just me and her and Eddy, the children already outnumbered the adults. But that didn't satisfy her. I remember one afternoon, driving around in her blue VW Bug — one of the modern ones with the bud vase on the dash — when I finally told her I wasn't sure I could handle that much change all at once, and that maybe she'd have to choose; a puppy *or* a baby, but not a puppy *and* a baby in the same year. At which point, Eddy cried out from the back seat, "Take the puppy, Mommy! Take the puppy!"

G is for Grief.

In 1969, Elizabeth Kubler-Ross wrote a book called *On Death and Dying* in which she posited that there are five stages of grief through which human beings generally move in dealing with death: Denial, Anger, Bargaining, Depression, and Acceptance. Her book represented a huge leap forward in the history of our thinking about grief, but as so often happens with genius, ever since then it seems that everyone else in the field has spent most of their time trying to figure out where and how Ms. Kubler-Ross was wrong. Current critiques point out that human beings never go through anything precisely in sequence, that people can be in two different stages en route to acceptance at the same time or go back and forth between them, and that others never get there at all. Fair enough.

Because Joan was sick for so long, I think I probably went through all these stages even before she died. In the beginning, I spent a lot of time in denial — encouraged by almost every doctor we ever talked to — and then later a lot of time angry too. I've always preferred the expansion of anger to the flattening out of depression — as Grace Slick sang, "One pill makes you larger, the other makes you small" — but I spent a hell of a lot of time crushed by sorrow as well. In fact, watching someone you love suffer for years is a kind of sorrow I never knew existed. It's relentless and punishing, and solitary too. It can only be indulged surreptitiously. The one who's going to live can't be extravagant about his misery. Not when the person who's dying is around. If your spouse is upbeat and hopeful, you damn well better be upbeat and hopeful too, no matter how hard that may be for you.

One afternoon in 2006, I got back from the office to find Joan, who was by then very ill, lying in bed with Frank, who was five at the time, both of them excitedly telling me about the BBC show they'd just watched about the formation of the planet. Apparently, at one point in the earth's early history, it had rained for a million years, and the idea positively thrilled them, the idea that it could really rain for that long. It made a big impression on me too, both the fact and the circumstances in which I learned it, and when I could — when I was alone — I wrote a song about it. I realize now, looking at the date, that I wrote it exactly one year to the day before Joan died.

when you go
december 27, 2006

the true story of creation is more humbling & profound
than anything we ever learned in sunday school
the earth was just a ball of fire
for half a billion years
then it finally started to cool
by then the moisture in the broken bits
of stars that formed the planet
had been spit into the atmosphere
when it finally cooled enough it started to rain
& man i'm telling you the truth it rained
about a million years
that struck me when i heard it
it made a lot of sense to me
about how long things take to cool
how long to heal an injury
when you go it's gonna rain again
when you go it's gonna rain again
when you go it's gonna rain again
about a million years

the truth is both more grand
and more indifferent to our wishes
than the stories that we tell
the meek inherit nothing
and the cruel do rule the world
and there's no heaven & no hell
there's just the endless
intertwining strands of accident & fate
that make up a human life
along the road you either realize your dreams
or lose your way
& maybe sometimes even lose your wife
i think of all the rainy days
before i stumbled onto you
i never dreamed of love nor mercy
you appeared the sky was blue
when you go it's gonna rain again
when you go it's gonna rain again
when you go it's gonna rain again
about a million years
you say it rained for 40 days one time
then life began again
well when this storm gets started
it will really be the end
when you go it's gonna rain again
when you go it's gonna rain again
when you go it's gonna rain again
about a million years

H is for Heaven & Hell.

The traditional idea of heaven is that it's the home of the gods and of the good after they die, just as hell is the realm of suffering and the place to which the wicked are condemned. Primitive man used to think heaven and hell were literally above and below the surface of the earth, but at this point in the march of knowledge, we've pretty much established that those spots are taken by the now-ragged ozone layer and what remains of our fossil fuels. Me, I don't believe that heaven and hell exist at all, other than — like angels — as perennial elements in the stories we tell ourselves. I take the psychoanalytic view that the reason they loom so large in our fictional cosmology is because they're simple and powerful externalizations of internal states of feeling that every human being knows from either ecstatic or devastating experience, just as the Hero's Journey is widely acknowledged to be an external representation of the internal growth life requires of every individual heroic enough to take on the task of actually growing up.

I'll tell you what I think heaven is like. The night I asked Joan to marry me, at Joss, the restaurant we'd gone to on our first date, I was so confident she'd say Yes that I couldn't help but wind her up a little. The dialogue went something like this:

>   CHRIS
> Sweetheart, I'm afraid we have to have a
> serious talk.
>
>   JOAN
> Is something wrong?
>
>   CHRIS
> No. Not really.
>
>   JOAN
>   (convinced there is)
> What is it?
>
>   CHRIS
> I've just been thinking.

JOAN

About what?

CHRIS

It's nothing to worry about.

JOAN

What is it?

CHRIS

Well, now, I'm not sure I'm catching you in the right mood.

JOAN

What?!

CHRIS

I think we should try and have that baby.

Sharp intake of breath. She reaches across the table to hug me.

CHRIS

Whoa, whoa, whoa.

JOAN

What is it, now?

CHRIS

Well, there's more to it than that.

JOAN

What do you mean?

CHRIS
I mean I can't just have a baby.

JOAN
Why not?

CHRIS
Because I don't believe in having babies unless you're married.

JOAN
(darkening)
Then why are we talking about this at all?

CHRIS
Will you marry me?

JOAN
(stops breathing, weeps)
Oh darling!

So if you think of heaven as the triumphant glee you feel the day you realize she'll say Yes if you ask her, you can think of hell as the desperate confusion of the day seven years later when she's terminally ill, heavily medicated, and wildly angry and she declares that she's moving out, taking the kids, and announcing to everyone who will listen that it's not so much the cancer but the stress of having you around that's killing her.

I is for Intelligent Design.

I don't know how some people can look out at the world and see evidence of Intelligent Design everywhere. I can't even look at the skyline of Los Angeles and see evidence of intelligent design everywhere. And when they start talking about the elegance of biological systems like the human body I just want to ask, what about cancer? What about when the cells go crazy and start dividing uncontrollably? What about the eyes and teeth and clumps of hair they find all jumbled up in tumors? And have you ever seen a picture of the ragged blood vessels a tumor will create to supply itself, in spite of the fact that its own growth will kill the host, upon whom it depends for survival? They look like they were drawn by one of those angry kids who used to wear hockey helmets in Special Ed. If Intelligent Design is really the culture's last reasonably respectable argument for the existence of god in the twenty-first century — and sadly, I'm afraid it is — I'm surprised there aren't more of us atheists around.

One Sunday morning many years ago, desperately hung-over at a friend's house in the Hamptons, I lay on the couch and watched a PBS documentary called the Circle of Revulsion. The phrase refers to the circle of grass around a cow pie, a few inches wide, that's too close to the feces for another cow to eat. There are millions of organisms in a cow pie that have just been dumped unceremoniously into the cold, harsh world, and have to get back into another cow's stomach to survive. So some of them form these phallic pistils all over the feces' surface — the grey fuzz that you see on a cow pie when it hardens — which gradually fill with fluid until they're swollen to the point of bursting. Others climb over each other in this great roiling mass to get to the top of the pistils before they pop. When they do, they send tens of thousands of these microscopic creatures flying in all directions. Most of them are doomed to land on the same cow pie again, but an infinitesimal percentage are flung far enough in just the right direction to land on a blade of grass outside the Circle of Revulsion and have a chance to be eaten by another cow.

Hmm. Mindless struggle, random outcomes, and the only meaningful reward a chance to survive a little longer? That sounds like real life to me.

Joan's experience with cancer started with a routine trip to the dermatologist, who noticed a worrisome spot on her face and biopsied it. It was malignant. She recommended a simple outpatient procedure called Mohs micrographic, or microscopically controlled, surgery. Of course, the surgery was substantially more elaborate than Joan had been told, and far more painful, and Joan took some time to heal, during which she wore enormous bandages on her face and would hardly leave the house. But eventually the bandages came off, and the dermatologist said she got it all, and there was nothing more to worry about.

A couple of weeks later, Joan finally admitted to the family doctor that she'd been in pain while trying to defecate for some time, and he sent her to an oncologist — just to rule out the possibility — and *she* saw something unsettling, and biopsied that, and Joan was diagnosed with anal cancer. (She hated the word. Anal. She often told friends she had colon cancer, which created all kinds of confusion when they'd get online and send her the latest promising research and statistics on a kind of cancer she didn't have.) Anal cancer is also a cancer of the skin but of an altogether different kind, far more virulent and aggressive than the spot on her face, of which her father had had maybe 40 removed over the years, although with a very impressive survival rate for the established protocol — a punishing combination of chemotherapy and radiation — at something like 90 percent.

I remember sitting next to Joan when she first got the news. She heard the oncologist out with no reaction, then said into the phone that she couldn't possibly begin treatment right away. She had a child starting a new school that week, and he needed her at her best. She could maybe start in October. I remember murmuring something like, "Sweetheart, you have to do what the doctor—" and getting waved off. Then watching in silence as she came to the same conclusion herself, after which she withdrew to the bedroom to be alone for a while. I heard years later from her friend Catherine that Joan called her that evening to say she had cancer, but that the playdate they'd arranged was still on. Catherine's son Ollie could still come spend the weekend with Eddy, so her long-planned romantic getaway with her boyfriend wouldn't be ruined. Catherine told me that story in tears the night after Joan's Memorial. She was sure she'd never have a friend like Joan again, a friend so thoughtful and selfless she could get crushing news like that and immediately want to reassure you that your own plans wouldn't be affected. I found the story moving too. I hadn't yet put it together that it was that same evening Joan went into her room and closed the door. I suppose it's churlish to wish that Joan could have shown me that same heroic kind of consideration — I'm sure it is — but I stood there staring at that closed door for quite a while, feeling lost and lonely and more than a little useless. All I wanted in that moment was to be with my wife whom I loved, and console her if I could, or maybe just cry with her about how unfair it all was. Apparently, all she wanted was anything but that.

J is for the Judgment.

People who believe in the next world often believe that things will finally be made fair there, that the righteous will finally be rewarded and the sinners finally punished. I dare say that's because here in this world, that's so clearly not the way it goes. Here, the selfish and greedy are rewarded disproportionately, while the kind and the generous look on in growing frustration, until the stress finally gets to them and they get sick and die. Or so it sometimes seems to me. In any case, I understand the wish to get credit for our many sacrifices that the first half of this fantasy represents, the fantasy that the righteous will finally be rewarded. Here in Hollywood, we're all obsessed with getting credit for our contributions, however small, and a lifetime of generosity would seem to warrant at least a separate card at the end of the show. But what about the other half of the fantasy, the darker half? What about the wish to see everyone else punished?

In a book called *The Drama of the Gifted Child,* Alice Miller writes about kids who are bright enough to internalize their parents' wishes for their behavior, who repress all impulses to behave otherwise, and become "good boys" and "good girls." Of course, this transformation comes at considerable psychic cost. Ms. Miller acknowledges that when these kids become adults, they can be very angry with people who haven't made this same deal, who haven't repressed these desires, who have instead indulged them — been grabby, egotistical, uncontrolled — and prospered. Is this the key to the fantasy? Is the aging child so anxious that other kids aren't being punished for their misbehavior — are instead being rewarded — that he or she needs constant reassurance that things will finally be made right in the end? I only ask the question because it seems to have had so much to do with our relationship, Joan's and mine.

Joan was every inch a good girl. She grew up the oldest daughter of two MDs in New York, where she went to Chapin and learned to curtsy. When her mom left her dad — they'd managed to marry, have affairs, and divorce, all without ever raising their voices at each other — and moved the kids to Chapel Hill, Joan was 12. Her mom started teaching a full schedule at the University of North Carolina, quickly developed an active social life, and was suddenly gone day and night. Joan took over as acting mom to her brother and sister, feeding them, helping them with homework, even sending them off to school in the morning in a taxi. The sight of one of them being delivered home by a Chapel Hill police car, having been forgotten after practice or a piano lesson, was not at all rare. Joan took over as her own mom as well. When it came time to apply to college, she did all her research on her own, and visited colleges as far away as California by herself. She wound up deeply angry at her mother, of course, but she was so well-bred that she almost never revealed her anger in public. With friends, she was so relentlessly cheerful that half of them never knew she was angry at all. Until she got sick.

Me, I'm the son of second-generation Italian and Polish theatre people who screamed at each other every day of my childhood. For reasons of self-preservation, I learned to be a good boy too. I went to Harvard and taught there. I wrote a movie about racism and justice that was nominated for seven Academy Awards. And once I got sober — and Joan had only ever known me sober — I lived up to all my obligations. But I was as angry as she was or more so, and a lot less well-bred about it. Her favorite movie was *The Philadelphia Story*. Mine was *On The Waterfront*. Got it?

So we had each spent our lives behaving well by the standards of our respective communities, and we were finding out that none of that mattered, that fate deals out its crushing blows with nary a glance at your résumé or your history of forbearance either, and we were starting to look around for an appropriate place to register our complaints.

K is for Keening.

Speaking of complaints, the word Keening nowadays suggests a kind of undifferentiated wail of sorrow, but once upon a time it was a more ritualized vocal lament over the body at a traditional Irish burial. The keen was made up of simple elements like the names of the ancestors of the deceased, and praise for him or her, and descriptions of how unhappy those left behind would forever be. Often a professional keener would lead, and be answered by a chorus of the rest of the attendees, who would rock from side to side and clap in time and when it came their turn sing their hearts out. In a thoroughly unsurprising development, the Catholic Church railed against the practice. The idea that a group of peasants might give what few coins they could scrape together to anyone other than the Church was anathema to the Cardinals of the Middle Ages, who were arguably among the most greedy and corrupt rulers in human history. They went so far as to threaten keeners with excommunication, and finally this lovely and sad group expression of grief died off altogether and Irish Catholics went back to just getting hammered at the wake.

Had I written a keen for my wife, I would've written that she was the best thing that ever happened to me. I must have told her that a thousand times when she was alive — even after she decided she wanted a separation — but she never quite believed me. She was the kind of person who dismissed extravagant compliments even in the best of times, and these were not the best of times. But it was true. She was the best thing that ever happened to me. You have to understand that I learned despair at a very early age, and I only learned hope when I met Joan. And I'm not talking about the words. I've always understood the words. I'm talking about the feelings: so powerful, so deep down, that they inform everything in your life. I remember my mother in the kitchen, standing at the dryer in her nightgown — there were days when she didn't bother to get dressed, and others when she just stayed in bed — wailing over and over, "I wish I were dead! I wish I were dead!" I remember standing in the doorway, at the age of five, stricken, knowing there was something I should do about this — about what I now recognize as her clinical depression — but not knowing what it was. I dare say this bottomless sense of my own inadequacy in the face of other people's pain has stayed with me all my life. In any case, if you had asked me what keening was a year ago, before I looked up its sad history, I'm reasonably certain that that's the sound that would have come into my mind: the high, thin wail of self-pity that my mother made.

I have only one other memory from childhood as vivid as that one. I remember looking down the long hallway in our railroad apartment in Manhattan in the middle of the night. I was maybe six by then, and supposedly asleep in the top bunk, but my parents were fighting and I was watching like a hawk. My mother was at the door, my father outside on the landing, but I could see his hand through the gap in the door created by unlocking it but leaving it on the chain. He was reaching in to try to get at her, and she was standing only an inch too far for him to do so, screaming that he was a drunken dago bastard and that he should go sleep it off on the street, while he screamed back at her that she was a spoiled bitch. Or words to that effect. The next morning, when I woke up and crept into my parents' room to see who was there — and who wasn't — I found them entangled in each other's arms, my father snoring heavily, and my mother with what I think was a black eye. But I'm not sure. I suppose I could have asked my older brother about it, but I never did.

In any case, from the moment I first considered the possibility, I knew I should never have children. I knew I'd pass on the alcoholic (paternal) and depressive (maternal) genes that I carried, and I also knew — or felt, certainly — that it wouldn't be fair to any kid to saddle him with me as a father. Until I met Joan, that is. When I met her, somehow all my negative judgments of myself and my tainted blood melted away. She seemed to me to come from another world, a world in which the habit of happiness was just as easy to cultivate as the habit of despair. She was so generous and hopeful that I was as generous and hopeful as I've ever been around her. I forgot about not wanting children because they might be like me, and instead I wanted them, because they might be like her.

Well, just about three weeks after we found out Joan had cancer, real cancer, anal cancer, three weeks during which my mother-in-law was virtually living in the house with us, three weeks during which I had ample time to think about the real possibility that my wife might die and leave me with four kids to raise on my own, I was in the kitchen making something for them one morning when I lost my temper and found myself shouting. And I wasn't shouting at fate, or at cancer, or at death, or even at my mother-in-law. I was shouting at Eddy, who had made some perfectly normal kid mistake the details of which I don't remember. But I do remember shouting at him, in a rage, then turning and punching the refrigerator. Then I recovered myself. And that was the end of it. Except of course, it wasn't. The faint marks of my knuckles are still there on the brushed aluminum panel on the front of the Sub-Zero. And by the next day, everyone on Joan's side of the family as far away as New York and North Carolina had heard about it, courtesy of her mom. I must have apologized to Eddy 50 times, and to my wife even more often than that. But some things you just can't take back.

L is for Loss.

A study presented at the American Society of Clinical Oncology determined that terminally ill cancer patients have a higher-than-normal divorce rate, but that it's almost always the healthy husband leaving the wife. In fact, I ran across a cancer survivor on the Internet the other day who wrote that in the 80s, when she was going through those same experiences, fully 76% of all the marriages affected by cancer ended in divorce. I have no way of verifying that number, but it certainly fits in with everything else I've read. Of course, most of those were also marriages in which the healthy spouse left the sick one. But it goes the other way too. My friend Gay, who also died of cancer last year — that was another kind of sorrow altogether — was in a support group at the Wellness Community here in West L.A. with a half dozen other women, and two of them — that's two out of six — had left their husbands as a result of getting sick, in part because they found that they who had been caregivers for years now needed caregivers and had husbands who weren't up to the task, and in part because, in light of the new presence of death in their lives, they were moved to reassess all their commitments. Death is like that. It makes everything else look temporary.

Me, I feel like I lost Joan twice: once when she left me, and once again when she died. In her opinion, the deterioration of our marriage was directly related to the deterioration of my ability to control my temper, as for instance in the episode with Eddy I described above.[3] My anger — or any vigorous expression of bad feelings on my part, really — had always filled her with a kind of anxiety that bordered on panic, whether it was directed at her or not. And when she got sick, she lost all patience for hearing me rant, whether about narcissistic directors, or the failure of the American experiment, or anything else. What had once sounded brilliant to her now sounded only bitchy and negative. And how dare I complain, when she'd worked her ass off all her life to be cheerful and got nothing for her trouble but cancer?

To me, of course, *that's* what the problem was. *That's* what was

---

[3] I'm acutely aware of the irony of me telling you what Joan's problems with me were, but here I daresay I'm on pretty safe ground.

at the heart of the matter. Cancer. At the time, that's all I could see; that the deterioration of our marriage proceeded in lock step with Joan's illness. When she was first diagnosed, I could tell almost immediately that she was looking at me in a strange new way, as if she were a female David Byrne singing, "This is not my beautiful husband." She denied it at the time, but I'm a child of alcoholics. I know when someone's looking at me like they wish I'd disappear. (And when I see that look, the Goodbye Look? All I know is to poke and prod and make it worse.) Years later, of course, Joan admitted that getting sick had led her very quickly to reexamine some of the bigger compromises she had made in her life — meaning presumably me — but at the time she denied it categorically.

Anyway, I found the experience of realizing that my marriage was not nearly so solid as I had thought just about as destabilizing as the news that Joan was sick. This may sound strangely naive to you, or just self-involved maybe, but I had never even considered the possibility that Joan might fall out of love with me before that. She once told me she loved me so much, if I died she wouldn't want to go on living. What had changed?

Well, as I've said, at the time I thought I knew the answer.

M is for Mortality.

In the introduction to a book of short stories called *The Continental Op*, Dashiell Hammett tells a brief story about having been hired by a woman in a small town in the Pacific Northwest whose husband had left her three years earlier. She had been hearing for some months that a man who looked just like her husband had taken up residence in a town about 50 miles away, and wanted Hammett to find out if they were true. Hammett found the man, who readily admitted having been her husband, and told this story about what happened. He had been happily married, and an insurance salesman, and he regularly walked home to have lunch with his wife. One day, as he passed a construction site, a girder fell and landed right in front of him, smashing the sidewalk and causing a bit of concrete to fly up and cut his cheek. He was stunned, and without ever really knowing why, instead of walking home he went straight to the bus station, bought a ticket to San Francisco, signed onto a tramp steamer and spent two years going around the world. When he returned to San Francisco, he was once again drawn to small-town life in the Northwest. He wound up living no more than an hour's drive from where he started, found a girl and remarried, and was selling insurance again when Hammett walked in the door.

I could see the power that the idea of mortality had over my wife, a power to unmoor just as great as the one that made the insurance salesman cut and run. There were moments when it was clear that it was the fear of death that provided at least the emotional power behind what eventually became her intense determination to be rid of me, moments when she was reminded that her time was short that could destabilize her and fill her with resentment. Moments like this one.

In the early summer of our last year together, when Joan had already made me move out, but I was still welcome, at her invitation, to come and stay the night sometimes, we were watching TV, and Joan had already started her elaborate preparations for going to bed. She was sitting in a bra but no shirt, having trouble attaching a bag to her stoma — the hole through which you defecate when you've had a colostomy — which was always angry and raw, when she heard the kids in the other room getting too rambunctious. She got up and walked to the door, saying, "Frank! Samantha! I want some peace! Now!" She poked her head into the living room for emphasis when she suddenly started to shriek, and retreated to the bathroom, "Jesus, god! I'm so ugly! I'm disgusting!" I hopped out of bed and walked towards her, stopping when I saw a long slender turd on the floor in the doorway to the living room. I said, "I've got it, sweetheart. Don't even worry about it." I got some paper towels and a Clorox Wipe from the kitchen and walked back to clean up when I heard Joan muttering curses in the bathroom, "I can't take it, you son of a bitch!" I asked, "Are you talking to me?" "Yes!" I looked into the bathroom to see that she was weeping, and dabbing at her stoma with a medicated pad. She shouted, "When you're not here, I'm fine! I can handle it! It's only when you're here that I freak out, for Christ sake!" I asked, "I'm the reason you're hysterical?" "Yes! Yes! A thousand times yes!" I said, "Sweetie, I'm just trying to help you." She screamed, "Well, it's not working! Is it?!"

She was right, of course. I just couldn't see it. Not yet. Anyway, just to complete my thought — my argument, my brief — about our relationship deteriorating in lockstep with her health, it was about a year and a half after they'd found the first tumor and Joan had gone through what we thought was a successful course of radiation and chemotherapy that they found the recurrence of the cancer. We were of course intensely discouraged. And Joan took another big step away from me. She started raising possibilities she would never have conceived of before, let alone verbalized; going back East to try to get healthy again, or taking the kids to Europe for the summer, or even buying a motor home and taking them on the road. Then some months later, she had a huge and disfiguring operation, which took three surgeons 10 hours to complete, and then all kinds of attendant complications during her recovery. By the time she was up and around again, we were arguing all the time. At first, it was almost always about what was wrong with our relationship — smart people can come up with the damnedest things to argue about when they want to — meaning whether it was my anger or the looming presence of mortality that was tearing us apart. But in the end, it was almost always about whether or not things would be better if I just left.

Finally, about a year after that, we were told she'd had a second recurrence, and literally before the week was out, amidst all the mortal dread and sense of defeat that news produced, Joan told me this was it. She wanted me out so she could concentrate on getting better. This time, she had her father fly out from New York to tell me she was serious, as if I couldn't tell myself. I moved to a friend's guesthouse where I stayed for two months, during which time the incident I just described above occurred. Then, when she decided that she had to get even more distance from me to have a chance to get healthy again, she moved into a rental house with the kids, and I moved back into our home.

Six months later, she was dead.

N is for the Netherworld.

To the ancient Greeks, Death was just the brother of sleep, there only to usher the dying to the river Styx, and it was the ferryman, Charon, who transported them across the river and into the Underworld. Theoretically, anyway. In fact, they never completely trusted Charon to do his job. They worried that he'd leave their dead suffering and lost on this side of the river, without a little extra incentive. That's where the custom of leaving pennies on the eyes of the dead originates. They also believed, according to

Herodotus anyway, that necrophilia was so ubiquitous amongst earthly undertakers that when beautiful women died, their husbands would let them rot for three or four days at home before sending them off to be prepared for burial, in order to make them less attractive to the embalmers.

Wow. I admit I was a little paranoid that the nurses might make off with Joan's jewelry (the nurses were great, I'd just heard about that kind of thing so many times on TV) but I wasn't worried about anything perverse. As it turned out, less than 36 hours after her death, Joan's rich brother walked me through her rental house and showed me all the things he said Joan had wanted him to take — which included just about everything of value she'd owned — then shipped it all back to himself in New York.[4] But that was about as perverse as it got.

Anyway, Joan died shortly after midnight on the day after Christmas, making it officially the 27th of December. The next morning, when I called the undertakers, Gates, Kingsley & Gates, the first words the funeral director said were, "This is the third call I've gotten about this person, from three different relatives! I should think someone over there would be able to decide who's in charge!" Jeez. What a start. I went over there that after-

---

4 At the time, I wasn't inclined to fight with him about any of his claims. I was and am disappointed by his behavior, but in AA they tell me to keep my side of the street clean, and leave it at that. Since then, I've tried to get a few of Joan's most valuable things back for my kids, including the original Miro print Joan's mother had given her, and her two Lawrence Carroll paintings, one of which I'd given her and the other Lawrence himself, but without much success. I'm afraid that's the way it goes sometimes though, when people die. Sometimes there's a mad scramble for "the stuff."

noon to make the arrangements, then later that day, three men in dark suits who unlike their boss were quiet and elaborately respectful came to take Joan's body away. They gave us a minute to say our last goodbyes, then put her into a body bag and a temporary casket. Everything went smoothly until they tried to wheel her out of her room and her dog, Silky, the Carolina dog I'd bought her after Piggy died, started growling. And she wasn't kidding. Her teeth were bared and she was growling quietly but insistently. She was warning them that if they took another step there'd be blood on the floor. We got her on a leash, and the nurse took her into another room until the undertakers got Joan outside. I followed them to the hearse, and I have to admit I wanted to tear them apart, too. On some deep animal level, I wanted to growl and drool and threaten just as much as Silky did. But I didn't, of course. I just watched as they slid my wife into the hearse — a big black SUV, actually — and took off. In fact, I stood there watching long after it disappeared.

Maybe the Greeks' mistrust of their own death-workers — supernatural and otherwise — was just another expression of the same primitive antipathy Silky and I both felt that day. Maybe it's just a natural visceral reaction to the men who finally take the person you loved away. Or maybe not. Maybe I'm just an angry, angry boy.

O is for Oblivion.

One of the things that most frightens people about atheism, I suppose, is the idea that after we die there's nothing. Emptiness. Oblivion. But that's not true. In fact it's egocentric to the point of being silly. After we die there's still life everywhere. It's just that we're not part of it anymore. Not as ourselves. We are as proteins and molecules, as useful building blocks to the rest of life — we'll have more to say about that in a minute — but not as the conscious entities we were when alive. It may be part of the atheist canon that it's our fear of oblivion that makes us embrace the various illusions to which we cling, but oblivion is an illusion too. It's a poetic conceit. It exists only in the imagination. In real life there's no such thing. Open the window and look outside. There's only this. There's only life, in which we briefly have the privilege of participating, then it's someone else's turn.

The first thing I did on the morning of Joan's death was get the kids together on my bed and tell them I had bad news. Frank knew immediately what it was. He knew his mom had died. And I'm afraid it broke his heart. The girls didn't really know what it all meant yet, but they could tell from Frank's tears — and my own — that it was very sad. I had each of the kids pick a flower from our backyard to take with them up the hill. When in Joan's bedroom, they put their flowers on her chest and kissed her goodbye. The girls had to be lifted up to do so, but Frank was able to reach her on his own. Frank was most deeply struck by how cold she was. It had been in the low 50s the night before, and her spacious but aging rental was never very well-heated, and she seemed to be as cold as ice to him. He mentioned it a couple of times. That's the action of Algor Mortis, the 'coolness of death' I mentioned above, the rapid cooling of the blood that begins as soon as the heart stops beating. I have to admit, it struck me as well. There was nothing that made it more clear that the person she had been existed no longer than how cold she was to the touch.

Other than that, I can't say I know how I felt in that moment. I guess I was pretty much on automatic during that period. I was okay when the kids needed help, and I was okay when I was working. The rest of the time I just kept my head down, emotionally and physically, and did whatever was required. I guess there were times when I wept. I remember being afraid that I might not get through Joan's Memorial without weeping, but I did. For my dad, it was something of a feat that he got through it without telling anybody off. He quit drinking himself in 1978, so by then he'd had just about three decades to practice not giving in to his darker impulses, and he managed to hold his tongue. But the Memorial was controlled for the most part by Joan's brother — who by then was pretty hostile towards me — so when you walked in to the friend's house where it was held, you were greeted by a blowup of Joan alone with her dog Silky, over her maiden name, Joan Muecke, and the years she had lived. Me, I knew it was going to be there. Hell, I had not only given her the dog, but I had given her family the picture to use. I knew how desperately they were looking for one that didn't have me in it. But my dad was surprised and offended at the way I was being written out of Joan's history. In fact, of the 10 or 12 people who spoke at the event, I think only one of them dared mention my name, and that was an old friend of mine who managed to make a mildly negative joke about me. Under other circumstances, that would have been fine. But under these, in which Joan was being remembered exclusively as an angel, as a perfect daughter, sister, mother, and friend, it stood out like a sore thumb.

But that's okay. I held my head up. When it came my turn, I

invited everyone over to my house for dessert and live music — my band and I played ten of the love songs I'd written for Joan over the years that afternoon, although only about half the people at the Memorial came — then I proceeded to make the few remarks that I had prepared. I closed by saying, "I've been a great admirer of Samuel Beckett's writing ever since I was a college student. He once summed up the entire pageant of human life in these words: 'They give birth astride of a grave, the light gleams an instant, then it's night once more.' Well, in my life? The light that gleamed an instant? That was Joan."

P is for Putrefaction.

Merriam-Webster defines putrefaction as "the decomposition of organic matter; especially the typically anaerobic splitting of proteins by bacteria and fungi with the formation of foul-smelling incompletely oxidized products." This clinical definition reminds me very much of Joan's dad, Dr. Muecke. He runs the largest urology practice in New York City, but he arranged to take a few days off to spend them with his daughter when she got sick for the third time, and the days stretched into weeks and then into months. I think he spent the entire last three months of Joan's life with her and the kids in her rental house. In the end it was he who pronounced her dead and noted the time and signed the certificate. Which was heroic of him. For a dad to watch a daughter die is brutal. The reason I'm reminded of him is that during that period, whenever I asked him how Joan was doing, he'd give me a detailed and accurate report on her medical status and the progress of her symptoms. He'd say, "Her breathing is increasingly shallow and the muscles of her eyes are no longer strong enough to hold them closed." He'd never just say, "She's dying and it's breaking my heart," although she was, and it was. In fact, he had a heart attack not two months after she died, although thankfully he recovered very quickly and was able to go back to work.

Much as death is more gut-wrenching than the good doctor could ever admit, so is putrefaction both more repulsive and more inspiring than the dry dictionary definition above. The moment a human being dies, bacteria that live in the intestines and feed on its contents start consuming the intestines themselves. The odor of decay these bacteria create is odious to other human beings, but attractive to blowflies — it's the aforementioned dinner bell — which lay eggs on all its openings. These eggs become maggots — the larval stage of the blowfly — and move into the body, feeding on the decaying tissues in a huge pulsating mass that warms the body again, often to interior temperatures higher than when it was alive. Later, wasps come and use the maggots and their warmth as living incubators, laying eggs inside them, which in their larval stage feed on the maggots until they're dead, then emerge from their carcasses as more wasps. Wow. If you can get past your gag reflex, you might see in that paragraph what I see in it, which is to say more tenacity, flexibility, teamwork, sacrifice, and determination to survive than there is in any six slacker movies. It's clear that in nature, there's no time to waste on mourning. There's no time to waste on despair or on judgment or on guilt either. Those are strictly human phenomena. In nature, there's only the most intense and immediate inter-species effort to turn death into more life as quickly as possible. In nature, there's only the baldest kind of determination to get on with it.

But I'm a complex organism — I admit it — and I need time to work through the kinds of life-changing and highly emotional experiences that human beings regularly have and that maggots and blowflies and wasps will never even dream of. I needed time to come to terms with my own obliviousness to my wife's emotional needs, for instance, with the fact that in her last few years I was acting out my own fear and confusion and despair half the time without realizing it and without being able to stop it and without taking into account how hurtful it might be to my dying wife. In fact, maybe I'm still acting out right now. Maybe all the off-putting imagery in this little book is really just more undigested anger. Maybe it's no more than an attempt to rub your face in it, to punish you for not having had to go through what I went through. I don't know. I don't think so, but I don't know.

I do know at this point that I'm not afraid of death. Not anymore. Not my own, anyway. And I'm not afraid to talk about death, either. I'm not afraid to talk about putrefaction, or embalming, or even autopsy. (The word "autopsy" is derived from the Greek, meaning "seeing for oneself." Gosh, I'm not only not afraid of seeing for oneself, I'm in favor if it.) What I am afraid of is pain. And I don't mean my own this time. I mean other people's. I'm still afraid of other people's pain and of my own stunted ability to assuage it, or relieve it — or even tolerate it — without being overwhelmed.

Here follow four examples of the consequences of my inability to respond to my wife's ever-increasing pain with anything but confusion, fear, and ultimately anger.

Q is for Quality of Life.

Quality of Life is a phrase most often used by people who know they're going to die and find out that one more operation, or one more infusion, or one more round of whatever devastating treatment they're on, might leave them confined to a wheelchair, or unable to see, or talk, or fornicate, or so dramatically weakened or damaged that the activities that they feel make life worthwhile are no longer possible for them. That's when they start weighing the extra time they might gain against their deteriorating Quality of Life. It's amazing how frightening their deliberations can be to the people who care about them.

When my wife started talking like this, I was terrified, and she did so very early on. We were en route to the USC Medical Center, stuck in rush-hour traffic on the 10, when she first mentioned it. She'd just been diagnosed with her first recurrence, and we were crushed. We were on our way to hear what the new doctors had in mind, and we knew it was going to be bad. We'd been told that for her kind of cancer, of the patients who undergo the brutal regimen of chemo and radiation she'd gone through the year before, 90 percent live cancer-free for the rest of their lives. What we didn't know at the time — what her father didn't tell me 'til the day after she died two and a half years later — was that of the 10 percent who have recurrences, no one lives more than five years. No one.

Anyway, as I've said, I was a middle-aged bachelor when I met Joan. Suddenly I had four kids — a stepson, a son, and identical twin daughters — and my wife was talking about refusing to undergo any more treatment for her deadly cancer. The idea that she might die and leave me to raise the kids alone scared the hell out of me, and like a lot of men I'm at my worst when I'm scared; my most pig-headed, my most controlling. Joan was pretty sure that whatever treatment the doctors proposed that day would be devastating. She insisted over and over that there was no guarantee that doing it would work, and who was I to tell her she had to do anything anybody said, anyway? I finally shouted that she might be right that there was no guarantee that the treatment would work, but that there sure as hell *was* a guarantee that *not* doing it *wouldn't* work, and that she might as well get out of the car right now and lie down in traffic as say she didn't want to try it!

Nothing like a screaming husband to make a girl in trouble feel loved.

R is for the Resurrection.

We've already talked about Heaven and Hell as externalizations of internal states. I dare say the story of the Resurrection is the same thing; a deliberately astonishing externalization of the internal story of becoming conscious, of coming to terms with reality, of waking up. In fact, there so many kinds of awakenings and reawakenings in the history of stories, from Osiris to Jesus to Sleeping Beauty to Rip Van Winkle to Kafka's Metamorphosis to all those silly Princes trapped in the bodies of frogs, that it's clear that the fantasy of starting over, of waking up transformed, or with the world itself transformed, is so deeply and profoundly human as to be virtually a defining characteristic of the race. Of all the creatures on the earth, we're the one that yearns to be reborn as something else.

When we first got married, Joan and I believed that we'd brought each other back to life. That's clear from the things we chose to read and say at our wedding. By five years later, though, Joan's idea of coming back to life had changed completely. By then, she had thoroughly conflated the idea of beating the cancer — of pulling out of this terrible vortex of fear and disease and anger and pain — with the idea of getting away from me. She literally told me two dozen times that she'd never get better if she didn't get away from me. Damn. I said a lot of terrible things to my wife during this period, but the one line I wouldn't cross — the one thing I never said — was that she'd never get better if she did, either.

I did tell her though that putting the kids through a breakup at this already miserable time in their lives was the worst idea I'd ever heard, and that I'd fight it in every way that I could. She reacted to that with some of the wildest things I'd ever heard her say. She accused me of having given her cancer, of only wanting to stay with her for the insurance money, and even of trying to kill her. I thought she was losing her mind, and I'm afraid I told her that too, more than once.

I wasn't the only one either. Her father Dr. Muecke also became concerned during this same period, having noticed quite a number of times that "her voice became slurred and incoherent" on the phone. He decided she had to be abusing the medications she was being given for her pain. Her brother heard this and immediately started arranging an intervention from his office on Wall Street. Oddly enough, I was the one who talked him out of it. She wasn't abusing her medications. They may have been affecting her judgment, but she wasn't abusing them. She needed every one of them for the constant pain she was in. Sadly, even though he gave up the idea of intervention, he still managed to let Joan hear about it, so she found out what her family thought of her wish to break up ours — that she was 'talking crazy' — and felt deeply and thoroughly betrayed. She retaliated by going public with every harsh word I had ever said to her, with every childish tantrum, with every empty threat. And more. Apparently, she said some pretty wild things to them, too, by way of persuading them that if they knew what I was really like, they'd want to get away too. She even demanded at one point that I call each of them and tell them she wasn't crazy, that in fact she was right — I was impossible to live with — which in a conciliatory moment I agreed to do. That made for some pretty silly phone conversations. I'm lucky her first husband and I got along as well as we did, because my efforts to explain to him that I was the only one to blame in my deteriorating relationship with his ex-wife made him laugh out loud.

Anyway, for my part, I can see how mean it was of me to tell my wife I thought she was crazy. What's more, I can see that she wasn't. She was desperate, but never crazy. Or if she was, I was too. I was so intent for so long on making her see how wrong she was to do this to the kids — and to me — that I was completely oblivious to the fact that all my attempts to argue and wheedle and shout her into changing her mind only made it more and more obvious that she had to get away from me if she ever wanted any peace.

S is for the Silence of the Grave.

Most people think of the grave as silent. But the grave is only silent because we make it so. In our efforts to keep putrefaction at bay, we fill our dead with chemicals and preservatives so off-putting, including formaldehyde, glutaraldehyde, and ethanol, that even the death beetles stay away. Were we not to do so, the grave would be teeming with life. Gosh, a group of university researchers in Australia left a half a kilo (about 1 pound) of raw beef out in the woods one time and came back 24 hours later to find 50,000 maggots feeding on it. That's not silence. That's a rock festival. In any case, there's another meaning to the phrase "the silence of the grave" that's actually more useful to us here.

One night, I was awakened by my wife's moans. She was in the bathroom. She'd been trying to defecate, which had been painful for her for a long time — this was well before her colostomy — so she tried to do it when no one else could hear. She'd sit on the john with a folded towel in her mouth, like Jerry Tarkanian, but not out of nerves, strictly in order to stifle her groans. On this night though, she wasn't stifling them. She was crying. I hurried into the bathroom, and asked her what was the matter. She turned and showed me. Her rectum had popped out, and her insides were now visible on the outside. I was horrified. I found out later that because the tissues and muscles in the area had been so massively irradiated and therefore weakened, while she was straining to defecate on this particular night, her rectum "prolapsed," which to a doctor is no big deal. But I didn't know that then. I only knew that she was asking me to help her put her insides back inside her, and I couldn't understand what she meant. You mean just push them back in? By ourselves? Yes, that's what she meant. I couldn't imagine doing such a thing. To me it was like being asked to sew a severed finger back on. I said we had to get her to the ER, but she hated the ER, as everyone who's had to go a disproportionate number of times comes to hate it. She wanted me to help her, and I couldn't do it. She finally figured out a way to do it herself.

In retrospect, I don't think she ever forgave me for that. Not for being unable to help her — she was always understanding about my weaknesses — so much as for that one brief moment when she saw horror in my face. I think it was in that moment that she decided I found her disgusting, and that that meant I didn't love her anymore. Which wasn't true in the slightest — I loved my wife until the day she died; in fact, I love her still — but which does bring us back to the other meaning of the phrase "the silence of the grave."

When you're in a conversation with someone dead, when you're trying to figure out where things went wrong, and how you could have hurt her so much, and whether or not you could apologize just one more time, the silence is deafening.

T is for Terminal.

Terminal is a word you don't want to hear in the doctor's office. And for that very reason, you don't hear it much anymore. Not if there's even the remotest chance you might live. No doctor ever used the word in Joan's presence or mine. Not once. (Joan still believed she would get better — or so she told our son Frank in my presence — nine days before she died.) They don't always tell you how long you have anymore either, even when they think they know. No doctor ever told us we had five years, or two, or even three months. Nothing. Modern oncologists are so acutely aware of the popular idea that mental attitude has a substantial effect on a cancer patient's prognosis that even though there's no conclusive scientific evidence to support the notion, they generally hesitate to do anything that might threaten a patient's often shallow reservoir of hope. Me, I wasn't always so considerate.

Joan had just gotten me to move out when she called in the middle of my Thursday night volunteer obligation to ask me to come home right away. It was an emergency. I raced home and found her on a mattress in the middle of the living room, shivering uncontrollably. She spent most of her time in bed by then, but she had decided she wanted to be a bigger part of the family life, so she'd dragged a mattress into the living room. Thankfully, the kids were elsewhere with the nanny and not seeing any of this. I got Joan to the hospital, where she stayed for the next five days, until her 104-degree fever was down. The next Thursday, she got me out of the same volunteer obligation with the same call. I got home to find her shivering on the mattress again, only this time on the phone to her friend Lucy in Michigan and — as she often was when talking to Lucy — wildly angry at me, in spite of the fact that she'd just begged me to come help her. And this time the kids were watching too, wide-eyed. I hunkered down beside her and said the first thing to do was to get her into her room, and she told Lucy, "He's trying to make me go to my room!" I heard Lucy on the other end of the line say, "Well, you don't have to do anything you don't want to do," and I said, "Of course she does, you boob. She's a mom."

And it was on. Our last big shouting match. I didn't want my kids to see their mom like this. I knew how long such an image could linger in a kid's mind. I'd seen my mother suffering when I was five and I still remembered it. Here were my kids — four and six — staring at their mom and having no idea how to help her, just like me. Frank literally told me as I walked him away that he was Doctor Frank and Mommy needed him. I told him "That's alright, sweetheart. A real doctor will help her." By all rights, she should still have been in the hospital — her fever was just exactly as high as it had been the week before — but both her parents were MDs, and I never saw a patient work a doctor better than she. Anyway, I got the kids out, and we argued bitterly. She was outraged that I thought I was in charge of anything she did, and I that she categorically refused to admit that she might be hurting the kids. Gosh, in the last two weeks, she'd already had a car accident (with Lucy in the car, no less! Why my heavily medicated wife was driving and Lucy was in the passenger seat I'll never know) and fallen down and broken a finger while home alone. From there to leaving a burner on, or the front door open, or a skateboard near the stairs, was just a matter of time. But she refused to acknowledge any of this. Which drove me crazy. I finally shouted that if she continued to ignore my concerns about the welfare of our children, we wouldn't just be separated. I'd divorce her and petition for custody. I said any judge in the country would grant it to me given the massive amounts of narcotics she was taking.

That did it. She spent that whole night on the phone, telling everyone we knew I'd threatened to have her declared an unfit mother. By morning, her brother and some other rich friends got together to hire 24-hour nurses — so I'd have no claim on the children — and to rent her a place of her own — so I wouldn't be able to bother her anymore.

If there was any one thing I said that I wish I could take back, I guess that was it.

Anyway, as painful as all of these memories are, I have to admit that the act of writing them down has at least helped me understand the behavior of some of my friends a little better. I started to suggest when I described Joan's Memorial how unpopular I had become in the more remote parts of her family — although not with her father, Ed, who had made a point of being around, and had seen what was really going on — but I don't know if I can really explain to you how many people I'd known for years dropped me altogether during this period. They heard I was threatening to divorce my dying wife, or conversely refusing to allow her to divorce me,[5] or whatever the hell they heard — no one's ever quite had the temerity to tell me[6] — and wrote

---

5 According to his lawyer, this is how Joan's brother justifies his behavior towards us since she died. Because I refused to grant my wife a divorce — which at my worst I'm sure I did at least as many times as I threatened to divorce her — he's refused as Trustee to give us any of the money from the Irrevocable Life-Insurance Trust we created, Joan and I, for the continuing welfare of the family. As we've desperately needed that money during these last three years of recession and a shrinking and changing movie business, that's been a terrible hardship for me and my kids.

6 As it turns out, I wrote that last paragraph two days ago, and I was talking to a friend yesterday about it, who said, "I'll tell you the one story I heard. I heard you had an affair, and that you had a framed picture of the girl you had an affair with and you put it up above your wife's bed so she'd have to look at it while she was dying." Oh, wow. First

me off with a kind of haughty finality that 'til then I had only encountered in fiction.

---

of all, I never looked at another woman, from the night of our first date until long after Joan died. Second of all... well, forget it. Joan's sister Anne was just visiting us a couple of days ago — this is months after I wrote that last sentence now — and told me that towards the end of our cohabitation, by way of a last-ditch effort to persuade her friends and family that anyone in their right mind would be desperate to get away from me, Joan started telling them I was abusing her. She had said the same thing to me a few times — that I was "clinically abusive" — but I had already heard worse from her in the heat of heated moments. I guess it just didn't occur to me that she might be saying the same things to other people, people who might be taking her literally. Anyway, that trumps the story of the photograph many times over.

U is for the Undead.

Remind me never to take sides in marriage again, okay? It's in fiction where monsters exist, not in real life. There are exceptions. There are Hitlers and Dahmers and O.J. Simpsons, and they dominate the conversation that is popular history. But in the normal run of life, most marriages don't have a hero and a villain. They're not James Bond movies. They're more complicated than that.[7] In fact, even James Bond movies are more complicated than that. You can make the case that even the simplest of stories that pit hero against villain rely for their emotional power not just on the boundless vanity of our capacity to see ourselves as heroes, but also on the fact that they're externalizations of the inner struggle between the "better angels of our nature" and the worse. At some level, we acknowledge when attending to stories what we can't afford to admit aloud: that both impulses exist within us: the heroic and the villainous, the generous and the shameful, the selfless and the cowardly. It's not that we're either James Bond or Dr. No. It's that we're both of them. That's why their struggle makes so much sense. We work out all kinds of internal conflicts in our stories, but most often we work through our fears about death. That's why so many of the stories that have lasted through hundreds and even thousands of years of human culture have directly to do in one way or another with the subjects of death, the dead, and the Undead.

The Undead is a word first used by Bram Stoker in his novel *Dracula*, to mean vampires. It's since come to mean all the fictional creatures who are dead but don't act like it: vampires, ghosts, and reanimated corpses of every stripe. Mary Shelley created a whole new sub-species of the undead in her novel *Frankenstein*, corpses brought back to life by science. Between

---

[7] By way of illustrating the point, the photo above was taken four days before Joan made me move out of the house. Now, does that look to you like a picture of couple that should immediately be separated?

them, the two novels have been stunningly influential, inspiring maybe 1,000 movies so far. In fact, I've seen one list of vampire movies alone that had 667 entries, so the real total might be even higher. In any case, it's clear that the fantasy of coming back from the dead resonates with people in all its forms: in religious stories, myths, fairy tales, novels, and horror films. Given the enduring power of all these stories — and taken together there are tens of thousands of them — I think it's fair to say that the human race's all-time favorite fantasy is the one of coming back from the dead.

Which I only mention here again because whenever we pass the fountains at the 3rd Street Promenade and I give my kids coins to throw in, they wish for Mommy to come back. I've never told them not to, but I must look a little pained when they do, because by the third or fourth time, one of the twins came over to me to say, "It's okay, Dad. I know she's not coming back. I just wish for it anyway." Well, don't tell anybody, sweetheart, but so do I. As bad as things got, there was still a lot of love between us. And in her last days, when she'd already stopped eating and her body was starting to feed on itself, when she was starting to look more like a Giacometti sculpture than the beautiful woman she'd always been, when half our friends had already decided I was a monster and they'd never speak to me again, Joan herself managed to forgive me.

V is for Vital Signs.

Vital signs are clinical measurements that indicate the state of a patient's essential bodily functions. The four standard vital signs are body temperature, pulse rate, blood pressure, and respiratory rate. The phrase "the fifth vital sign" generally refers to pain, as perceived by the patient on a zero-to-ten scale, but many doctors reject this on the grounds that a patient's assessment of his own pain is subjective. There is no agreed-upon "sixth vital sign," but among the contenders is emotional distress, although doctors who won't take your word for it about pain probably won't waste a lot of time worrying about your level of emotional distress either.

My wife was almost always in pain in the course of her battle with cancer. The first time they found a tumor inside her it was the size of a BB, but located in a painful spot. By the time the first recurrence was diagnosed it was the size of a baseball, and even more poorly located, near the base of her spine, at a confluence of many hundreds of nerve endings. When it was removed in a massive operation requiring 10 hours of cutting and sewing, it was the size of a ham, and in order to get it all, the surgeons had to remove her bladder, her uterus, her rectum, and most of her vagina. Between the last recurrence and the day she died, it grew rapidly, doubling in size every two months, invading most of her remaining organs including her lungs, and eventually breaking through the skin of her back, so it was visible from the outside.

To manage the pain, she went from morphine to the fentanyl patch to dilaudid to the lollipop, back to morphine, then to a combination of drugs, one for constant pain and another for breakthrough pain, always in higher and higher doses, always at the cost of "increasing sedation and disorientation" (the family doctor's words, not mine). She changed pain doctors two or three times. By the end, she was taking nerve blockers, and couldn't feel anything in the lower half of her body, and with that, she finally found relief.

In terms of emotional distress, things took a similar course. She was always good-spirited — I was the difficult one — until she got sick. After that, I remember her shouting at me once, *"I want to be the crazy one for a while! I want to be the crazy one!"* (I just looked at her in that moment and thought, "And so you shall.") But in her last weeks, when her physical pain finally subsided, she managed to find herself emotionally again too, and she was once again willing to see me.

Of course, part of that had to do with the fact that I'd already undergone a big change for the better in terms of my own emotional distress. There had been a time when I was obsessed with the idea that she was wrong to break up the family, and that that meant that I was right. (It didn't.) For weeks after she moved into her rental house, I railed to friends on the phone about how wrong-headed and unfair it all was. Then one day I stopped. I don't know why. I guess I finally realized that if I wanted to have any relationship at all with my wife in her last months on earth — and I did, I desperately did — I'd better stop judging her and instead start asking her if there was anything I could do to help. I don't know how much of an impact this change in my attitude really had on her or on anyone else, but I know I felt better, and that must have been reflected in the way I behaved. Let's face it. The burden of being misunderstood is enormously heavy — it's the weight of the world, as they say — and the simple act of setting it down is an equally enormous relief. So enormous, in my case, that I was finally able to forget about my own pain and remember once again how much I loved my wife. Had I not done that, I don't believe I would have been invited back into her life.

I guess I finally realized how angry I was, too. After ranting on the phone every day for weeks — it literally took me that long — I suddenly heard myself. I heard myself the way my friends must have heard me, the way my wife must have heard me, as a self-absorbed, self-righteous, and relentlessly self-justifying son of a bitch. Damn. I always knew I could be a prick, but I never once expected to end up like this. Was it possible that my anger had really been the thing that had ruined my marriage? Was it possible that my wife's cancer had both triggered and exacerbated what had been a long-dormant or at least slightly-better-controlled-back-then anger problem? One that maybe I'd been controlling with vodka and cocaine for years without realizing it, and then had finally let flower in sobriety?

Shit. There are steps along the path to self-knowledge that I hate. I really do.

I have to tell you, I'm just lucky I married Joan. Not only had she put up with me longer than a lot of other women would have, but in the end, and mostly just to be kind to a desperately sad and frightened man, she took me back into her heart.

Anyway, here's another song I wrote for her, years and years ago, in a far far happier time, when I felt much more confident that I knew who she was and what she wanted — and that I could maybe provide it — than I ever did once she got sick.

i know the beat of your heart
july 11, 2001

i know the beat of your heart
i know the sound of your dreams
i know just where to start
to provoke your faint screams
i know the curve of your shores
as you lie there awake
i know the silk in your drawers
i know how much you can take
i know you hide hopes that you'd like to see real
& i know just what they are
you think you've concealed the way that you feel
but i see behind all your pale scars
i know the beat of your heart

i know the beat of your heart
i know the sound of your dreams
i know you've been torn apart
i've seen all of the seams
i know the width of your walls
i know the depth of your lakes
i know each horse in your stalls
i know what riding them takes
i know you hide hopes that you'd like to see real
& i know that you think that i'm scared
you think you've concealed the way that you feel
but i wouldn't be here if i didn't share
every beat of your heart
every dream in your eyes
every wish in your stars
& all the love behind your disguise
i know the beat of your heart
i know the beat of your heart

W is for Will to Live.

Recent studies have shown that the will to live in the face of terminal illness is depleted more by psychological factors than by physical ones — meaning more by depression, hopelessness, and a sense of futility than by pain. In fact, having a specific goal can have a disproportionate influence on exactly how long a dying person survives. Old people regularly live long enough to witness the birth of a grandchild, for instance, and we've all heard stories of parents injured in accidents and natural disasters surviving just long enough to deliver their children to safety. It even happens in showbiz. Gower Champion directed the revival of his own hit Broadway musical *42nd Street* at the ripe old age of 100, and managed to put off dying until opening night, making it possible for the producers to announce his death at the final curtain, make headlines in all the New York papers the next day, and virtually guarantee the success of the show.

In spite of her earlier flirtations with the idea of giving up treatment, in the end my wife's will to live was immensely strong, and based primarily on her profound attachment to her children. The fact that she made it through Christmas was no accident. It was a Herculean act of will. She wanted the kids to have a nice holiday, so she was going to live through it, no matter what. Her family was not as sanguine as she and moved the gift-giving celebration to the 23rd, to be sure she would make it, but they needn't have. They didn't always seem to know how willful Joan was. Her dad did, but the rest of them didn't.

Dr. Muecke spoke to me about her stubborn streak once, but only once, a few days before she died. He was in a reflective mood, and had had a glass or two of wine, and he started talking about the "Muecke women." He told me a story about his mom, who decided to take her kids back to Germany from America just two years before the start of World War II. All kinds of people told her not to — that there would soon be war, that people were fleeing Germany, not returning to it — but she wouldn't hear a word of it. She had decided she was taking her children back to the Fatherland, and that was that. So young Ed suffered through his childhood and early adolescence in Germany, until the end of the war.

I guess he was trying to explain his daughter to me by telling me this, to explain why she decided to break up the family in spite of the fact that the kids would have to go through first that dreadful experience and then shortly thereafter their mother's death. But as I've said, Joan never thought of what she was doing in those terms. She really believed that if she could just get away from me, she would live. Besides, what her father didn't know was that I'd already come to terms with her decision, and that she'd already forgiven me my ugly reaction to it, and for that reason I didn't need to hear such stories anymore. But I thanked him for telling it to me anyway. It was generous of him to do so. His daughter was dying in the other room, and here he was taking the time to make sure I didn't feel too bad about everything that had happened. I guess it's not too hard to tell where Joan's extraordinary generosity of spirit came from.

Which reminds me that just about a month before she died, on November 21st, in fact, according to my notes, Joan told me that the reason she had wanted us to live separately was so that I would be prepared to live without her when she died, which was not at all true, but which was also a remarkably generous thing to say. Generous and heartbreaking at the same time. It brings tears to my eyes to read it right now.

X is for X-Rays.

When William Rontgen discovered the X-ray, he was so excited he stopped eating, stayed in his lab, and repeated his initial experiment over and over for weeks, until he was sure of what he had. Finally, he brought his wife Bertha in, and showed her a picture of the bones of her hand, expecting her to be delighted. Instead, she saw what she thought of as a terrifying premonition of her own death, and ran screaming back into the house. I love that story, in part because he seems to have understood his wife even less well that I did mine, but also because he was so excited to be able to see deeply into the heart of things, no matter what was revealed. To most people, that's a decidedly mixed blessing.

On the day Joan was to move out of the home we had shared since our second date, she was released from a four-day stay in the hospital. She could have gone straight up to her new rental house — it had been spruced up, painted, furnished, and all her things moved into it while she was in the hospital — but she called and said she was coming home first. When I met her car in the driveway, she got out of the back seat and fell into my arms. She was walking with a cane at the time, and weak, but that's not why she fell into my arms. She just wanted comfort while she cried, and told me that she had to do this for her health, that she was only going for six months until she got better, then she was going to come back, and that she was sorry for hurting me. I told her not to worry about me, that she was doing the right thing (which I didn't believe, of course, but the last thing she needed right then was for me to give her a hard time) and that everything was going to be okay. I invited her in. When she asked me to grab her bag, her mom, who was at the wheel, said, "Don't touch that! We're not stopping here. We're going to the new house," but Joan told her to stay out of it.

I was rehearsing with my band that afternoon, and I had warned them that if Joan got home while we were still working, we'd be playing love songs exclusively. So we did. We played her four or five of the 30 or so love songs I'd written her over the years. And when the kids got back from the park, they did just as I had asked them to do if they came home and Mommy was here.

They started dancing to the music. Only they really got into it. They pranced around with their arms in the air like little Deadheads, and they were absolutely hilarious. When I looked over at Joan, tears of joy were streaming down her face. It struck me then that this was everything she had ever wanted: a house full of kids, a husband playing her love song after love song that he'd written for her, and everyone together having a good time. Only it was all fucked up, too. She was dying, and moving out in what was at least in part a desperate act of denial, and I was broken-hearted and resentful, however well I was behaving that day. And don't forget, her mom was still out in the car, snarky and brooding, eager to move things along. At one point, I watched her sneak across the patio, peer through the glass doors behind Joan, see that her daughter was having a good time, and retreat in disappointment to her car. But still, Joan was crying tears of joy.

Now to me, that's a real moment in a real human life, in all its terrible shame and glory. And getting you, the reader, here to this point, equipped to understand the bittersweet wonder and horror of this particular moment in this particular life, is as much as any other single thing the reason I wrote this book.

Y is for Saying Yes to Life.

Tolstoy had a dream which he describes in the introduction to a little book he wrote called *A Confession*, in which he found himself staring up at the night sky in peace, when he suddenly started wondering where he was and what was supporting him. He started to look around, and was alarmed to find that there were only two leather straps, each about four inches wide, one under his shoulders and the other under his knees, and that not only was there below him a bottomless and blank abyss, but that the more he tried to move around and see what the straps were attached to and whether or not they could be relied upon to continue to support him, the more precarious his position became. He finally realized that he had to stop trying to figure out what was holding him up and go back to staring up at the night sky again, because it was only then that he had felt safe. With that, he woke up.

Tolstoy interpreted this dream as meaning that he should convert to Catholicism. As far as I'm concerned, he couldn't have been more wrong. To me, it's much more profound than that. It's about the relief that comes not with the abandonment of reality in favor of faith (which in Werner Herzog's brilliant definition is "that peculiar human ability to believe in things which are not true") but instead with the acceptance of the limits of our ability to know. To me, the willingness to accept not knowing why things are the way they are is at the very heart of the search for inner peace. And that's a hard place to get to. It's a lot easier to give in and believe the same primitive stories our ancestors believed than it is to accept that while our first task is always to come to terms with reality, we'll never in our lives understand it.

But that's what happened to me. It took a while — in fact, it really took until long after my wife passed away — but I got there. I don't know why Joan fell in love with me. I've been tempted a thousand times to think it was the biggest mistake she ever made in her life. But I don't think that anymore. I don't really know why she left me either, although I have some ideas. Sadly, they have to do with my deepest character defects — anger and self-pity — defects it took me years to even acknowledge — I guess my capacity for denial is even greater in sobriety than I'd thought — and will yet take me years more of work to fix.[8] And for the life of me, I'll never know why she got sick and died. That still hurts. And it always will.

But I'm no longer suffering about what happened between us. I've come to terms with the fact that I have a lot of work to do on myself before I can go around blaming anybody else for how they behave. Least of all Joan. She was in a fight to survive. She was doing what she thought she had to do to live. Who can blame her for that? She wasn't an angel — I said in the beginning of this book that she was widely considered to be one, but that's not quite the same thing, is it?[9] — but she was great. She was terrified towards the end — maybe even wrongheaded, I don't know — but she was heroic, too. She packed up her kids and took them off to start a new life when most people would have packed it in. And in her last days, she was as graceful and generous and forgiving as she had ever been. She stopped worrying about whether or not admitting that she still loved me

---

8 I'm going through a workbook called *Anger Management for Dummies* with my therapist right now. And taking antidepressants as well. Apparently, irritability is very much associated with depression.

9 I just learned yesterday from Joan's sister that in her last weeks on earth, Joan was finally honest with her mother about all the ways in which she'd been a disappointment as a mom. I understand that this conversation — argument, fight; I don't know, I wasn't privy to it — took several days, and was profoundly destabilizing to her mom, who when it was over left Los Angeles and her daughter behind. Mind you, I don't say this to discredit Joan. In fact, I don't blame her in the slightest. I think she was settling accounts. I think she was cleaning house.

committed her to anything anymore — how could it? She was dying — so she admitted it. And to my great relief, she forgave me all my desperate efforts to make her stay the person she had used to be. She was a real woman in every possible way, and I'm so glad I fell in love with her and went through all this with her that I can't even say.

Z is for the Zombies Who Don't.

So there you go. Throughout history, man's been determined to deny, in countless of his culturally significant but scientifically dubious pronouncements, from the Bible to the Koran to the Vedas to L. Ron Hubbard's *Dianetics*, the one undeniable fact of life everywhere: the fact of death. And yet death still stalks him every day, in his fantasies and in his campfire stories, in his dreams and in his waking moments. It stalks him with the plodding gait of the zombie. It stalks him with the supersonic grace of the F22-A. It stalks him with the silent but relentless determination of the uncontrolled division of cells.

As I write this, on a Saturday morning, I'm thinking about how to tell my kids their grandmother died yesterday, Joan's spooky mom, also of cancer. We were going to visit her in New York during spring vacation,[10] but we were too late.

I'm just glad Joan forgave me before it was too late. I was visiting a week or so before she died, and I apologized yet again for all my churlish behavior, which since I'd stopped being quite so churlish I did all the time, but this time she looked me in the eyes and said... well, here. This is from an email I wrote myself that day, just — I don't know — to make sure I'd heard her right. "She just told me, at 5 p.m. on the 21st, that she wished she could do it all again. I told her Me, too... She looked in my eyes and said I can tell from your face that you love me." And with that, I was forgiven. It was a small thing — the earth turned infinitesimally beneath our feet, as it always does — and yet everything changed. After that, she let me visit every day. I sat with her and told her what I was working on, and what our friends were up to. I told her I loved her with all my heart so many times that she wanted me to have that inscribed on the back of the watch she wanted for Christmas — "To Joan, I love you with all my heart, Chris." For that, as it turned out, we didn't have time.

---

10 I suppose I should tell you she never once called here after Joan died, not to check on her grandchildren, or to chat with them, or even to wish them a happy birthday. When we heard she was sick, I decided to take the kids to see her anyway, but we didn't make it in time.

I did have time to play her one more love song on the guitar. She was pale and weak in her last days, and in no shape to be too demonstrative about her enthusiasms — a hand fluttering up off the covers and hovering in the air a few seconds before she set it back down was her most eloquent gesture — but her eyes were still bright, and her smile still lit up the room. Or so I imagined. Maybe her smile only lit up the room to me. I don't know. But I played her this song — the last love song I wrote for her, two months before she died — several times that week, and she loved it. She told everyone she spoke to about it. Until one day she woke up and she couldn't speak anymore. And the day after that, she couldn't see. And then the day after that she was gone.

We close our shows with this song sometimes, me and the band. My son comes up on stage and sings it with me. You should hear it sometime. It has a great ending.

everything whispers
october 15, 2007

everything mumbles & everything lies
everything crumbles & everything dies
everything fades & then everything's gone
everything's leaving it's all moving on
but darling I need you to get through the day
everything out there agrees you should stay
everything's nodding the trucks & the trees
everything wants you to stay here with me

everything's asking the sprinklers the lawn
the empties the ashtray the TV the dawn
the hiss of the streetlights the hum of the road
everything's talking cause everything knows
darling I need you to get through the day
everything out there agrees you should stay
everything's nodding the trucks & the trees
everything wants you to stay here with me

everything's sorry & wants to atone
everything's scared it'll end up alone
everything's changed & it wants you to see
everything wants you to stay here with me

everything wonders what more it can give
everything whispers it wants you to live
everything whispers it wants you to live
everything whispers it wants you to live.
everything whispers it wants you to live
everything whispers it wants you to live.
(repeat ad infinitum)

Afterword

I want to say something more about my kids before I go. I moved my office home to be around as much as I could when Joan died. I never thought I could write in a house full of kids, but I guess I was wrong. My office is in my bedroom now, and the kids sleep in here a lot: Frank in the big bed with me, Samantha on a mattress on the floor, and Julia on a bed of folded covers between the mattress and the bed, which is bizarre to me but pleases her enormously. When I wake up at six and start writing, I'm surrounded by my sleeping children and I love it.

The thing is — and people rarely say this kind of thing out loud, for obvious reasons — their lives settled down dramatically when their mom died.[11] They left the hysteria and fear and the constant presence of death behind them in that rental house — where for instance my son had had wild tantrums almost every day and often refused to go to school — and came back to this very orderly and very patterned existence down the hill, and they're flourishing. We've driven by the rental house a couple of times since then. The first time we went up there, it had already been demolished. The second, a McMansion had been framed up in its place, which made for an appropriate period at the end of a long and terrible sentence.

We all miss Eddy, of course. He lives with his dad, who moved back from Puerto Rico to take care of him. We see him when we can, but it's hard. He's 16, and an A student, and a *World of Warcraft* enthusiast, so he has other things to do. I worry about him, because he hasn't really talked to anybody about his mom's death. The little kids have been going to a grief group at a place called Our House every two weeks for two years — I didn't give them a choice — but Eddy told his dad he didn't want to do anything like that.

Me, I tried to get into the spouses' group at Our House myself, but when the lady in charge heard we'd been separated for six months before Joan died she told me I didn't belong in the spouses group,

---

11 The picture above was taken the day Joan died. I had contacted a woman who ran a grief group at a nearby hospital, who wanted me to bring the kids to meet her before their mom passed away, so I made an appointment for the following week. As it turned out, Joan died the night before the appointment, but we went anyway. It seemed like the right thing to do. I took this picture in the hospital garage that morning. I've stared at it many times since then, trying to see if I can find any sign of the knowledge of death in it, but I can't. Unless it's just the protective way Frank seems to be holding onto his sisters. As I've said, he's the only one who understood what had happened.

but that I could be in the friends' group if I wanted. I probably could have explained to her why I thought that even though we were separated, we were still very much married, but somehow I didn't have the energy in that moment. I guess I wrote this book instead. Which I'm tempted to say was a much more difficult experience than group therapy could ever have been. But I don't really know.

Most people take refuge in made-up stories to escape the sorrow and finality of death. Let's call the writing of this little book an effort to take refuge in reality. In so far as that's what it was, I'd have to say it worked. Having struggled with it for some time now, I think I can honestly say that just getting through it, just having to collect and clarify my thoughts, admit my failures, and come to terms with the inexplicable and the ugly in the world and in myself, has been rewarding on a level that I don't think any kind of escape can ever match.

It's also my way of saying one last goodbye to my beautiful wife, Joan, whom I love, and always will, with all my heart.

Goodbye.

PS: I'm including one more love song I wrote for my wife. I don't know why. I guess just because she liked it.

you are my home
january 17, 2006

wherever i go on these 18 wheels
i remember you are my home
on i-99 into bakersfield
or that icy road to nome
you are my home
you are my home
you are my home

whenever i stop in a cheap motel
buy a toothbrush & maybe a comb
i think why i drove until darkness fell
& how far these wheels have roamed
you are my home
you are my home
you are my home

wherever i am at the end of the day
if i know where i'm going or i lost my way
you are my home
you are my home
you are my home

we could be swimming on an island in greece
man we could be living in rome
i could be writing my masterpiece
i'd still be reciting this poem
you are my home
you are my home
you are my home
you are my home

Photos

The cover photo was taken by Kramer Morganthau on the set of the pilot for *Over There*.

The picture of my kids at letter D was taken by me with my iPhone.

The picture of Joan with Silky at letter O was taken by a very good professional photographer called Andy Comins.

The picture of Joan and me at the letter U was taken with a cellphone at a dinner party but I can no longer remember who took it.

The picture of Joan carrying Frank at letter V was taken by Andrea Williams.

The picture of all four kids at letter W I took with my iPhone at Eddy's new home in Malibu.

The picture of my three kids the day after their mom's death I took with my iPhone.

Chris Gerolmo is a writer, filmmaker, and musician. He wrote *Mississippi Burning*. He wrote and directed the HBO movie *Citizen X*. With Steven Bochco, he created and executive-produced the FX series about the war in Iraq called *Over There*, directed the pilot, and wrote and sang the Emmy-nominated title song. His first album *I'm Your Daddy*, his second, *Live on Brave New Radio*, his third, *g.o.d. loves you*, and two EPs, one called *Man on Fire*, and another of five songs he wrote for his wife called *a record for Joan*, are all available on the internet. Chris lives in Brentwood with his three kids, Frank, Samantha, and Julia. His stepson Eddy moved in with his dad.

www.ingramcontent.com/pod-product-compliance
Lightning Source LLC
LaVergne TN
LVHW041256080426
835510LV00009B/759